Techniques in Business Credit Management

Techniques in Business Credit Management

R.D. "Rusty" Rutherford

Publishing Division

National Association of Credit Management
475 Park Avenue South, New York, N.Y. 10016

Library of Congress Cataloging in Publication Data

Rutherford, R.D.
Techniques in business credit management.

1. Credit — Management. I. Title.
HG3651.R77 1984 658.8′8 84 — 18965
ISBN O-934914-58-3
Manufactured in the United States of America

First Printing

Dedication

This book is dedicated to Raymond H. Richards, former vice president and treasurer of Geosource Inc., who chose me as his company's first manager of corporate credit. Ray's love of credit management coupled with his unceasing search for extraordinary and excellent performance in himself and his subordinates challenged me as no one has before. My task for him was not only to install a credit system for this new company but to develop the best credit system that could be built anywhere.

This credit system, Ray insisted, must be built upon fundamental, unchanging credit truths. To that end, he gave me great flexibility and latitude to visit the credit operations of other companies, attend the Graduate School of Credit and Financial Management at Stanford University, and work closely with other Geosource managers, especially those in the Treasury Department.

Ray insisted that his managers not only be excellent in their specialties but be excellent managers of people and the resources made available to them. Although he did not teach or coach directly, he introduced us to situations and exposed us to close scrutiny by experienced professionals so that we learned what was required of a generalist manager.

While Ray was a stern task master and accepted nothing but the best that was, in his view, possible by anyone, he showed me how substantial a benefit an excellent credit function in a company could have on that company's bottom line, and the high degree of personal satisfaction that a credit manager could gain from that accomplishment.

Ray has since retired from Geosource but I hope he will continue to stimulate others in credit management as he has me.

R. D. Rutherford
Houston, Texas

About the Author

R.D. "Rusty" Rutherford is the credit manager of the Oilfield Services and Rental Unit of Weatherford, U.S., Inc., Houston, Texas. The National Association of Credit Management has bestowed upon him its coveted title of Accredited Business Credit Executive.

He has received the Fellow Award from the National Institute of Credit and the Executive Award from the Graduate School of Credit and Financial Management, which he attended at Stanford University.

Mr. Rutherford is a member of the Houston Association of Credit Management. He has served on the board of directors of the NACM Oklahoma Division and on the board of governors of NACM Wisconsin.

At the Oklahoma association, he was education chairman and taught courses in business credit management in Oklahoma City and Tulsa. He now teaches in Houston.

Before joining Weatherford, Mr. Rutherford served in positions of increasing responsibility for Geosource, Inc., which he joined in 1976 as its first corporate credit manager. He has been credit manager of the company's Geolograph Pioneer Division and has helped form a new Wireline Services Division for the company, serving as its first credit manager.

Mr. Rutherford was born in Chicago. It was there that he was introduced to credit management by Dun & Bradstreet as a city credit reporter.

After graduating from the University of Wisconsin, he joined Gulf Oil Corporation and then Interlake Steel Corporation. Several years later he became corporate credit manager of General Fire Extinguisher Corporation. While at General, he helped form a new National Fire Extinguisher Manufacturer's Trade Credit Group through the Chicago-Midwest Credit Management Association.

In 1972 he joined NCR's Appleton Papers Division as credit manager. Four years later he moved to Houston to join Geosource.

NACM

The National Association of Credit Management is a member-owned and controlled organization of 87 affiliated local associations in the United States and an international subsidiary that operates in Europe. The NACM was founded in 1896 to promote good laws for sound credit; protect business against fraudulent debtors; improve the interchange of credit information; develop better credit practices and methods and establish a code of ethics. In addition to those original objectives, education and research programs illustrate NACM's awareness of the complex needs of credit management today. Membership in an NACM-affiliated credit association includes membership in the National Association of Credit Management. Members of the NCAM are credit and financial executives, primarily representing manufacturers, wholesalers, financial institutions and varied service organizations. Membership now exceeds 45,000. For information regarding membership, write to executive offices: 475 Park Avenue South, New York, N. Y. 10016.

Contents

Exhibits

Introduction

Techniques in Business Credit Management has been written to introduce the new person in credit to the work of a credit manager in a logical way. Many times instruction to newcomers in credit is abrupt and disjointed because the credit manager attempts to train his people on-the-job while answering the telephone, talking to visitors or conducting the myriad of short and varied tasks that make up his busy day.

Having worked in credit since 1961, I can assure new credit representatives that they can truly learn the ins and outs of the credit profession only by approaching the material in a logical and systematic way. It takes time — a great deal of personal time away from the work place — and hard work.

I encourage you to write in this book. Underline, highlight, add or cross out. Write out questions in the margins and discuss them with your supervisor or fellow credit managers. Your credit work is too important to your customers, your company and your 1
career to take anything for granted. Do anything you must to make this book a working document for you. Don't be fooled by the seemingly simple statement that sounds obvious. Most credit managers get in trouble because they overlook the implications of the obvious or forget the basics.

Some credit managers using this book to train their staff may wish to emphasize or add points they feel are particularly relevant. I encourage you to do so. I have deliberately omitted discussion of those credit subjects which can be discussed only in the context of unique company management practices, financial considerations or industry environments.

Some may wish to substitute their forms for those presented. Be my guest!

Any suggestions for improvement of this book as an introduction to business credit management will be personally acknowledged by me. You may address me at: Rusty Rutherford, Credit Risk Management Associates Inc., P.O. Box 772597, Houston, TX 77215.

There are many credit subjects I have treated very briefly or omitted. The section on financial statements is an example. I have not attempted to intensively discuss the intracacies of these documents. What I have attempted to provide is an introduction to these mysterious documents, which totally overwhelm the newcomer. If I have only raised questions that stimulate further investigation, this chapter will have served its purpose.

Similarly, I have not delved into the various methods credit managers use to determine the dollar amount of a particular customer's credit limit. That amount is determined upon aspects unique to a particular situation both in the customer's environment and the credit managers' company environment.

This book is organized into 10 chapters, each focusing upon a particular area. I encourage you to approach each chapter in sequence as each builds upon the other. The language is kept deliberately informal since most of you will be reading this after putting in a full working day.

Some people have told me that credit is an art rather than a science. While the importance of the style of the credit manager cannot be underestimated (hopefully, it will be the subject of my next book), there are fundamental guiding principles of credit management that have rung true throughout the years. These principles form the foundation for *Techniques in Business Credit Management.*

I also do not want to imply that anyone can become a credit manager by simply reading a book. Neither you nor your company can give yourself the title of credit manager. You must earn this title by exhibiting your knowledge, skill, managerial ability and compassion for people, earning the respect of your customers and co-workers in the process.

Finally I wish to thank three marketing vice presidents who have shaped my style of credit by their approach to the problems we faced and solved together: Harold House of Gulf Oil, Bob Knapp of NCR, and Darrell Williams of Weatherford. The last chapter in this book is a result of their strong belief that credit management is and can be a positive profit-contributing force in any company.

Rusty Rutherford
Houston, Texas

P.S. You may wish to turn now to the last section in the book called Important Terms for Credit Managers and make note of any unfamiliar terms. You'll become acquainted with these terms as you read through the book.

Chapter 1

The Philosophy Behind Credit Transactions

The title of this chapter might be expanded to read . . . The Philosophy Behind Credit Transactions or Why Do We Need Credit Managers At All?

Credit can be defined simply as "the ability of a person or business to buy now and pay later." Using this as a definition, we are able to say that a person or business has "credit power" or "credit ability." This capability is usually measured by the track record, which indicates ability and willingness to pay bills.

The ability to pay may best be judged by a thorough review and investigation of available financial background information such as financial statements, profit and loss statements, jobs or work in progress or, in the case of individuals, sources of income, including salary, rents, commissions, etc.

There is no way to truly determine willingness to pay, except to anticipate that your customer will pay in the future as he has in the past.

Today, many people think that businesses extend credit. The truth is credit managers accept the credit power of people and businesses by approving deferred payment and allowing goods and services to be purchased without immediate payment. This approach gives the credit manager several advantages:

1. The burden is on the person requesting credit acceptance to prove that his credit is acceptable by furnishing sufficient financial information, plus names of trade suppliers and banks who have previously accepted his credit.

2. Credit ability is a measurable and limited resource. If a person lacks the income to pay credit billings, that can be determined in a rational way by reviewing paychecks. You may find that his credit has been used up or is simply not any good. Credit approval is thus based upon facts, not the whim of the credit manager.

In short, then, *credit* is the power to purchase without paying immediately.

Business credit is a technique used to increase sales by offering customers deferred payment. So much for the textbook definition. In modern business, most companies must offer at least their standard industry (usually) net 30-day terms to the majority of their customers to remain competitive. Offering terms beyond the industry standard is the credit tool used to obtain increased sales, and in today's economy it is used quite often.

Business credit is also characterized by substantial investment in customer selection. It has been estimated that it takes at least five sales calls to set up a new customer. The cost for these calls has been estimated in excess of $500, so before a firm makes this kind of investment, it simply makes sense to determine whether there is at least a reasonable possibility that the customer will have the ability and willingness to pay.

The credit department will often be asked to perform a preliminary credit check before the salesman makes additional sales calls after the initial customer contact. Information to be given the credit department for the credit check should include:

1. The legal name of the entity that will pay the bills.
2. The address where billings are to be mailed.
3. The telephone number of the business.
4. The name of the principal owner or officer.
5. The amount of credit requested and the terms of payment.
6. The potential purchases for the next 12 months.
7. The amount of profit margin in anticipated sales.

8. The names of suppliers who have accepted the customer's credit, and the names of the customer's bank.

With this information, the credit manager will most likely order a credit report from several sources:

1. Dun and Bradstreet (D&B)
2. National Association of Credit Management (NACM)
3. Specialized Industry Reporting Services

The credit agency report is the initial starting place because its cost is quite low compared to the time it would take the credit manager to develop the information himself.

Dun and Bradstreet

D&B, probably the largest credit reporting agency, produces a report that is the basic starting place for any credit investigation. From records on file, D&B first confirms the customer's identity. If the firm is a corporation, that is, an organization authorized by a state to conduct business, with liability limited to the amount of assets contained in the organization, D&B will check the State government office that authorizes corporations to do business in that state. Then, unless they have a current file on the company, D&B will send out a credit reporter to interview the company and determine the following:

1. The owners or officers of the firm, their background or antecedents.
2. The type of business: retail, wholesale or manufacturing.
3. The operations of the business, that is, what the business does to make money.
4. The territory of the markets served by the business and the number of its customers.
5. A list of suppliers who have sold the firm on credit.

6. The name of the firm's bank.
7. A current financial statement for the firm.

The information obtained from the owner is then confirmed by the D&B credit reporter by telephoning or interviewing references and checking legal records.

This report is accessible by computer (if the company is on file) in about a minute. A great starting place. Contact D&B for the costs of this report.

National Association of Credit Management

NACM is a non-profit trade association of more than 45,000 credit managers. NACM reports contain only the results of past payments of the customer with suppliers and are usually available by computer. The reports are available for a fee. Contact your local association for details.

The NACM report contains the following information:

1. Trade style.
2. Address.
3. How long sold.
4. Date of last sale.
5. High credit. The highest amount owed by the customer at any one time, usually the prior 12 months.
6. Current amount owed.
7. Current amount past due (beyond terms).
8. General manner of payment (prompt, according to terms; slow, shown in increments of 30 days.)

Specialized Industry Reporting Sources

There are agencies servicing a specialized industry. In general, their reports are similar to those of NACM associations.

Based upon the information in these reports plus the information supplied by the salesman, the credit manager can give a preliminary approval or let the salesman know what additional information is needed to accept the credit of a potential customer.

Many credit managers classify customers based upon their apparent credit risk and anticipated payments. A coding scheme I have employed is as follows:

A	Prime	Good credit risk. Expect payment in 30 days.
B	Good	Good credit risk. Expect payment in 30-60 days.
D	Marginal	Potentially a good risk. Expect payment in 60-90 days. Company has the potential to be upgraded to the B classification within 90 days.
E	Business Risk	Customer lacks the potential for an immediate upgrading. Management has weighed the potential revenue and the apparent risk, and has decided to sell to this customer.
Y	Cash Only	The credit risk and the limited potential require all purchases to be prepaid.

A credit limit is then assigned, which represents the maximum amount of the customer's credit the credit manager will accept at any one point in time, and the credit manager sets up a credit file, which becomes a permanent record for the particular customer. This file folder contains the credit reports obtained, any sales call reports made by the salesman, the results of the telephone reference check by the credit manager and the Credit Limit Approval Form, which documents the credit limit and risk code assigned to the customer.

In developing these credit codes and the accompanying credit limit, the credit manager often uses what are called the 5 C's of Credit to make certain all facets of a credit investigation are covered. The 5 C's are as follows:

1. *Character.* This aspect considers the customer's reputation, primarily past payment record. Like the other C's, character is based on facts, not the credit manager's intuitive feel of the customer's honesty. It is determined by comparing the customer's payment record with others and by checking legal records for suits, judgments, etc.

2. *Capital.* This concerns the customer's ability to pay. It can be determined by reviewing the financial statements.

3. *Capacity.* Capacity or capability involves the ability of the customer to run his business at a profit. Does he know his markets, competition and product? Does his management team have the skills to effectively manage the business?

4. *Conditions.* What is the economic environment the business must operate in? What are the interest rates, product maturity and competition?

5. *Coverage.* Does the business have proper insurance coverage to ensure its survival in the event of a catastrophe?

While the 5 C's are often criticized as being too general, the areas they cover serve as a good basis for any credit investigation. Each area must contain facts which answer the following basic questions:

- Does this potential customer have the ability to pay ultimately and the ability to pay within the terms of payment we intend to offer him?

- Does this potential customer have the willingness to pay within the terms of payment we intend to offer him?

Until these two questions can be answered with reasonable certainty, the credit investigation should continue.

At this point, we will discuss the most important, and ideally the only form a credit department should require from potential customers, the *credit application.*

The credit application is the document the customer uses to describe his business to the credit manager. It is from this document that your relationship with your customer develops.

Should we require customers to fill out an application? Legally it makes sense. If we can show in court that a customer has requested credit, we probably stand a better chance of collecting what is owed us. More importantly, if the customer requests in writing that we accept his credit, he is entering into a contract with us. This commitment often means we will be in a better position to be paid than others who do not have such a formal agreement. Therefore, it is to your advantage to obtain a written and signed application from your customers. It makes sense also to print your company's standard terms and conditions on the reverse side of the application so your customer is familiar with your expectations. (We will go into the credit application in more detail in Chapter 2.)

We have now briefly covered what credit means, how it arises, why a credit manager conducts a credit investigation and how credit risks are classified. At this point, it is also important to discuss the principals of credit information exchange among credit managers.

Credit Interchange

Credit interchange is the exchange of credit information about customers between credit managers. The NACM has worked very hard to keep credit information on a very high and ethical level to protect customers from abuse by unethical credit managers. In individual conversations with other credit managers or at meetings to exchange payment experience about common customers, NACM credit managers adhere scrupulously to the following rules:

1. Always convey facts not opinions.
2. Restrict information to ledger experience or facts of past experience limited to confirmation of name, address, telephone number, name of principals, date account opened, date of last sale, high credit, balance now owing, amount past due, age of past due and gen-

eral manner of payment. (Under general manner of payment, you may indicate the following: pays within terms, pays slow XX days, placed for collection, first sale, no payment experience, prepayments our request, prepaid by customer option and no recent experience.)

3. Do not recommend how others should handle an account and do not speculate on future account handling.

4. Retain all credit information in confidence and do not disclose specific comments to others in your company, *especially the sales department.* The information could be quoted out of context. Other departments would probably not use the information with a credit manager's sophistication.

On the next page is a sample worksheet for a credit investigation of a new customer:

NEW CUSTOMER CREDIT INVESTIGATION

DATE	INQUIRY FROM
LOCATION	TELEPHONE
AMOUNT OF FIRST SALE	ESTIMATED DATE OF FIRST SALE
ESTIMATED SALES WITHIN 30 DAYS	CREDIT LIMIT REQUIRED

LEGAL NAME & INVOICING ADDRESS		PURCHASING NAME & PURCHASING ADDRESS
TYPE OF BUISNESS (CORP., PART. PROP)	DATE STARTED (YEARS IN BUSINESS)	BRANCH OF

PERSON TO CONTACT FOR PAYMENTS		PERSON TO CONTACT FOR PURCHASE ORDERS	
NAME	TELEPHONE	NAME	TELEPHONE
TITLE		TITLE	

BUSINESS REFERENCES (COMPANIES WITH WHOM CREDIT HAS BEEN ESTABLISHED)

NAME	ADDRESS (INCLUDING ZIP CODE)	TELEPHONE	DATE LAST PURCHASE

RESULTS OF REFERENCE CONTACTS

SOLD SINCE	HIGHEST AMOUNT OWED	TERMS OF SALE	PAYING RECORD	NOW OWING	PAST DUE	INFORMATION GIVEN BY

BANKING REFERENCE

NAME	ADDRESS	TELEPHONE	PERSON TO CONTACT
CHECKING	SAVINGS		LOAN OWING $
ATTN			

RESULTS OF BANK CONTACT

ACCOUNT SINCE	BALANCE AVERAGE	LOANS UNPAID AVERAGE	SECURED / UNSECURED
PURPOSE OF LOANS			INFORMATION GIVEN BY
GENERAL COMMENTS			

13

Chapter 2

Investigating New Customer Credit

In financial terms, a credit manager manages a portfolio of investments for his company. These investments are the amounts due from customers who have promised to pay **not immediately but later.** The credit manager's job is to accurately predict when these amounts will be received so his company can use the cash for purchases, payrolls or investment.

Predicting anything is not easy. Some people say credit managers develop a "feel" for their customers and can predict fairly accurate payment trends by gut instinct. It stands to reason that the longer you are a credit manager, the more easily you will be able to make predictions. That is probably due to the fact that you have mastered the processes and principals of your craft and are applying them without realizing it.

Most decisions in credit should be based on fact because of the tremendous impact they can exert. For example, your customer's survival may very well depend on your accepting his credit. Likewise, holding shipments or suspending credit can create a serious impact upon the fate of many companies. Therefore, credit managers can't afford to guess.

When approving credit, a credit manager should be willing to commit his company's resources to a particular customer only when he has the facts demonstrating that the customer has the financial ability to pay according to the payment terms offered him.

The first step, then, in the credit investigation is to contact the customer and obtain some basic information. When these facts are confirmed by outside sources, the basis for accepting the customer's credit is established. Fundamental facts include:

1. Name of legal entity responsible for paying bills.
2. Address where invoices are to be mailed and any special billing requirements.
3. Name and telephone number of individual to contact if there is a problem.
4. Composition of legal entity (proprietorship, partnership, corporation, joint venture, trust). Date started. Source and amount of working capital. Assets. Outstanding obligations. Principals or officers and their antecedents or backgrounds.
5. Companies who have accepted credit of the entity and their credit terms. Amount presently outstanding.
6. Name of bank and account officer. Outstanding obligations.
7. Amount of credit your customer is asking you to accept. Products and services he intends to purchase. The desired terms of payment.

This information can be gathered verbally, but to speed transmittal it is usually presented on a *business credit application*. Since the application is the credit department's initial contact with the customer, it should be well designed with sufficient space to complete all the information. It should also contain a space for the title of the person giving the information, his signature and the date. Your company's standard terms and conditions[1] of purchase should be printed on the reverse side of the form.

---

[1] Conditions of sale will vary from company to company. By developing uniform conditions of sale and reproducing them consistently in quotations, credit applications, price lists, catalogs, invoices, acknowledgements and statements, the customer is presumed to accept them unless indicated otherwise in the document. Because of their importance, these standard terms should be drafted by a qualified lawyer. Their content should include any area of potential disagreement, especially where terms conflict with normal trade customs in your industry. Some areas might include: terms of payment (where, when and in what currency); F.O.B. point; payment of freight; policy toward returned material; who pays taxes or packaging; warranties; insurance coverages; and payment of interest on past due balances.

The most important point is that these standard conditions, once developed, should be reproduced consistently on all important documents, especially the credit application, quote, price list or catalog, acknowledgement and invoice. For the instrument to be effective, the customer must be given an opportunity to review and object to any terms and conditions before the sale is consummated.

The credit manager is now in a position to confirm the credit information he received from the customer. In choosing his information sources, the credit manager will consider:

1. The accuracy of the information given by the source.
2. The speed with which the source can give information.
3. The cost involved in obtaining the information from the source.

In Chapter 1, we said that credit agency reports are often the first credit source chosen by the credit manager. While the reports rate high in speed and cost, they are often not as accurate as direct contact with the source.

When contacting credit sources directly, the credit manager first prepares for the call. The source will want to know the reason for the inquiry and some basic identification about the customer. Most credit inquiries go like this:

> "Hello Mr. Jones. This is Rusty Rutherford, Credit Manager of CRMA. Donald Smith of ABC Company is asking us to open up an account for him. He is requesting a credit line of $50,000 and has mentioned that you are presently selling his company on a credit basis."

> "Yes, Rusty. Don Smith has been a customer of ours for over three years. His recent high credit has been $10,000 although ABC has owed us over $100,000 in December of last year. Presently, he owes us $5,000 which is current within our terms of net 30 days. All payments to us have been made as agreed."

Occasionally, things will not go so well and the credit manager must probe:

> "Hello Mr. Jones. This is Jack of CRMA. My credit manager told me to get a credit check."

> "Well, Jack. Who do you need a check on?"

"Oh, its ABC Company."

"Where, Jack, are they located?"

"Oh, I don't have that written down. Don't you sell ABC? They said you did."

"Well, Jack. We have several ABC Companies and I want to give you the correct information. Why don't you check your records and call me back?"

Fortunately, most credit people are more prepared. Now, let's see how a credit manager would report derogatory information.

"Yes, we do have an account established for ABC Company. We've sold them for the past six years, but last month we had to decline further credit until their past due balance is paid. They owe us $14,000 from February, which is three months overdue on our terms of net 30 days. They have promised a partial check for $2,000 each week beginning next Monday."

Notice that the credit manager merely reported the facts, easily proven. No opinion was given as to whether he thought the customer would pay under the proposed schedule, nor were there any comments of outrage since the customer didn't pay as originally agreed. You may want to review the principals of credit information exchange presented at the end of Chapter 1. To be a professional, you must adhere to these principals.

Contacting other credit managers is called a trade clearance by direct inquiry. The same information can be obtained from D&B, NACM or other specialized reporting services, although the information may not be as accurate since a third party is used to gather information. The information also may not be as current since most agencies only collect information periodically.

When the company you are investigating is new or payments to others are unsatisfactory, you may wish to contact the customer's bank. Before contacting the bank, be certain you have your facts straight. To gain the most from your bank inquiry, be prepared to share some of your information with the banker. It is also best to plan in advance what you wish to learn and to contact the customer's account officer at the bank rather than the bank credit department.

A typical inquiry goes like this:

> "Good morning, Mr. Thompson. This is Rusty Rutherford, Credit Manager of CRMA. George Jessel of RWR Oil Company has asked us to contact you. We are attempting to open a normal trade account for George and we anticipate monthly purchases of $25,000 on terms of net 30. George indicates your bank provides the primary financing and that a loan of $300,000 is outstanding secured by accounts receivable and inventory."

By sharing information in this detail, the bank account officer is reasonably assured George has given you as a reference and is now in a position to confirm this information to you. The banker's reply could go like this:

> "Yes Rusty. We have had an account for George under RWR since September of 19XX. His depository account is a medium six figures and is satisfactory. We granted a medium six figure loan in April on a secured basis. Presently outstanding is a moderate six figures and the loan is being paid as agreed. We consider George to be a valuable customer of the bank."

Bankers and credit managers have developed standards for credit information exchange called the *Robert Morris Associates Principals of Credit Inquries*. A copy is shown on the reverse side of the Request for Bank Information on page 24.

Once the credit manager has contacted the trade and bank references, he may, to be thorough and to avoid grief later, confirm the telephone number and address in the telephone book or in lists published by industry trade groups. If a large amount of credit is requested, he may request financial statements from the customer or obtain them from a broker if the customer is a public company. (We discuss financial statements in Chapter 8.) Only when these facts are gathered is the credit manager in a position to approve the acceptance of the customer's credit and to document that decision with a *credit limit approval form.*

The credit limit approval form documents the assigned credit limit, the risk code and the approved terms of payment. Documenting the decision ensures:

1. The sales department knows what payment terms they can offer and whether or not they should ask for a larger credit line.
2. The manufacturing and operations departments know what credit check requirements are on repeat orders.
3. All personnel in the credit department know what decision has been made by the credit manager. In the event of a change in personnel, confusion should not result. Also, the same documentation can be used to enter information into the computer (which we discuss in Chapter 9).

The astute credit manager should not overlook the information the salesman can offer. Most credit managers want to know both their immediate and potential credit exposure. There is nothing more embarassing than to approve a nominal amount only to be required to go back to the customer two weeks later because of the increased amount of credit involved in a subsequent purchase. In addition, the salesman can tell the credit manager how important the account is to the company's marketing program. (It may provide a valuable outlet where the company has no representation.) In this case, the credit manager may attempt to approve a larger credit line than normal, even in the case of a marginal account.

Mature companies involve their credit manager with the sales department during preparation of a sales forecast in the budgeting process. Restrictive credit terms may limit sales to specific customers thus invalidating the sales forecast. If this is the case, the credit manager and the sales manager should jointly develop a strategy to sell the particular customer the desired volume in a prudent manner.

Following are samples of a business credit application, a trade inquiry and a bank inquiry:

Business Credit Application

Credit Risk Management Associates Inc.
P.O. Box 772597, Houston, TX 77215

Customer Legal Name ______________________________

Billing Address ______________________________

City/State/Zip ______________________________

Type Organization __________ Date Business Started __________

Telephone __________ Principal Name __________

Supplier Name	Address	Telephone No.	Last Sale

Bank Name	Address	Telephone No.	Officer

Amount of Credit Requested $__________ Terms __________

In consideration of your accepting the credit of my company, I agree to pay all invoices within your terms of sale as printed on the reverse side. In addition, I agree to pay a service charge equal to the legal maximum rate in our state for all invoices unpaid after your terms. You may contact the references given in order to appraise the credit of my company.

Information Supplied By:

____

____

Signature and Title Date

Trade Inquiry

Mr. John Jones
Credit Manager
ABD Company

Our Customer: Credit Risk Management Association
Houston, Texas

Dear Mr. Jones:

Our mutual customer has applied to us to open a new account. We estimate monthly purchases will run $25,000 on net 30-day terms.

Would you please give us the benefit of your experience together with any comments you feel would be helpful.

All information will be kept in strict confidence and we will be glad to give you our experience at any time. A postage reply envelope is enclosed.

Sincerely,

Rusty Rutherford
Credit Manager

Date Sold From ______________________

Date of Last Sale ______________________

High Credit (Last 3 Mos) ______________________

Now Owing ______________________

Past Due ______________________

Oldest Invoice ______________________

General Payments ______________________

Comments ______________________

Bank Inquiry

Mr. Jason Smith
Vice President
Texas National Bank

Re: Credit Risk Management Association, Inc.
P. O. Box 772597
Houston, TX 77215

Dear Mr. Smith:

Our mutual customer has applied to us for a credit line which we estimate to be about $25,000 monthly on terms of net 30 days. He has given your bank as a credit reference.

Would you give us the benefit of your experience with our customer. All information will be kept strictly confidential in protected credit files.

Thank you in advance for your help. A self-addressed envelope is enclosed.

Sincerely,

Rusty Rutherford
Credit Manager

Customer Since ______________________________

Depository Account Balance ______________________________

Loans Outstanding ______________________________

Monthly Payments Amount ______________________________

Term ______________________________

Security Held ______________________________

Manner of Payments ______________________________

Comments ______________________________

Note: Any written inquiries to a bank must contain an original signature of the credit manager, not a stamp or facsimile. Many banks prefer use of the form shown on the next page and will respond more promptly if this form is used.

REQUEST FOR BANK CREDIT INFORMATION

Please provide bank credit information on the account below. This information is requested for use in the extension of credit for business purposes only and will be held in strict confidence. We are providing a summary of our experience with the subject of the inquiry.

SUBJECT: ____________________
(Company on which inquiry is made)

____
(Street Address)

____
(City, State, Zip)

TO: ____________________
(Bank Name)

____
(Street Address)

____
(City, State, Zip)

____
(Date)

FROM: ____________________
(Your Company Name)

____
(Street Address)

____
(City, State, Zip)

____
(Inquirer's manual signature)

____
(Print or type name of inquirer)

____
(Inquirer's title)

INQUIRER TO COMPLETE THIS SECTION

The purpose of the inquiry is:

☐ Initial order $ ____________________
Anticipated requirements $ ____________________
☐ Established customer; increased requirements to $ ____________________
☐ File revision.
☐ Change in payment experience from ____________ to ____________
☐ Other (describe) ____________________

We are referring this inquiry to you because:

☐ Your bank was given as a reference (provide branch/account no. if possible) ____________________
☐ We are checking with other area banks and information from your file only will suffice.
☐ Other (describe) ____________________

Our experience with the subject has been:

Sold since ____________ Amount Owing $ ____________
Last Sale ____________ Terms ____________
High Credit $ ____________ Amount Past Due $ ____________
Collateral (describe) ____________________
Are there guarantees, endorsements? ____________

Our file contains:

☐ Current trade credit reports.
☐ Financial statement dated ____________
Year end ( ) Interim ( )

The last time we made an inquiry of your bank on the subject was ______
Comments ____________________

24

BANK TO COMPLETE THIS SECTION

Our experience with the subject has been:
Depository accounts: Date(s) opened ____________ Average Balances ____________ If closed, when? ____________
Aggregate balances used? ☐ yes ☐ no
Experience and comments ____________________

Loan Accommodations: Describe, including length of borrowing relationship, high credit, types of loan accommodations (line of credit, term loan, mortgage, installment, etc.), amount outstanding, amount past due (if any), collateral, guarantees and endorsements (if any).

____

Loan Experience/Comments: ____________________

Financial Statement: Date ____________ Period Covered ____________ Audited: ( ) yes ( ) no

NACM

rma

This form and the "Statement of Principles" (See Reverse Side) have been approved by the Robert Morris Associates and the National Association of Credit Management.

____
(Manual signature of banker)

____
(Print or type name of banker)

____
(Banker's title)

____
(Date)

To be submitted in duplicate.
Bank to retain one copy.

Form 19
Additional copies may be obtained from
NACM, Publications Division, 475 Park Avenue South,
New York, N.Y. 10016

Chapter 3

Reducing Risk from Marginal Customers

Marginal accounts, customers who have a tendency to pay slow for whatever reason, usually comprise a significant portion of any company's receivable portfolio. In fact, most firms could not survive unless they cultivate the business of marginal accounts. The credit manager's job, then, is to manage these accounts successfully.

In dealing with a marginal account, the first step, of course, is to recognize that you are selling just that, a marginal account, customers we classify as "D" or "E" credit risks. From trade reports and conversations with other credit managers, you may learn that your marginal customer pays slower than normal. Hopefully you may also learn the reason for his slow pay. Is it prudent to sell this customer on the extended terms he has implicitly proposed?

Your first decision is to predict whether or not the customer will survive. Serious under-capitalization, lack of management discipline, overzealous selling or extremely competitive industry conditions with resulting pressure on profit margins will be some of the facts you will consider. Will this customer be *able* to pay at all?

Secondly, you must determine whether payments to the trade are consistently slow or erratic. If payments are consistent, you can accurately predict the loss in profit margin your company will sustain if you sell the account on credit terms. However, if payments are erratic, the business may be out of control and it will be extremely difficult for you to manage the account. Is the erratic payment due to the financial condition of the company or the owner's attitude toward paying his bills?

Next, you must consider whether a rehabilitation program can be designed to bring the customer to a prompt paying condition. This may mean personal discussions with the customer to sell him on prompt payment as a way of securing your company's line of products or to suggest alternative terms such as consigned inventory or assignment of sales with a commission paid after you receive payment from his customer. You may wish to consider offering special terms for a limited period to help your customer solve a temporary cash flow problem.

Marginal accounts are changing constantly. To keep up with the changes you will have to spend a greater portion of your time on these accounts. Your salesman must also be prepared to spend additional time to help you monitor this account.

It might be helpful for you to do what I do when dealing with marginal accounts — apply the National Safety Council's defensive driving formula:

1. Recognize the hazard. Be alert to identify a potential or existing customer as a marginal account.
2. Know the defense. Possess the knowledge you will need to know to protect your company from potential loss.
3. Act in time. Marginal accounts change rapidly. You must establish a monitoring system and use your field sales people as sentinels to alert you to changing conditions. Also, you cannot procrastinate when making a decision regarding a marginal account. Most marginal accounts aggressively seek to have their credit accepted since many companies will refuse them credit facilities. Most salesmen and top managements when faced with extreme pressure and indecisive subordinates will choose the path of least resistance — and that means you will be working to collect the marginal account you didn't approve.

Let's now consider some of the defenses you can employ to protect your company from potential loss from sales to marginal customers.

The easiest method, often overlooked, is to shorten your normal terms. If you usually offer net 30 days, offer net 10 and insist on prompt payments. This reduces your exposure by one-third and lets you evaluate payment performance three times a month instead of once a month.

Another method is making use of the personal continuing guarantee. This is a document the customer executes guaranteeing payment to you if the company doesn't pay. In effect the person is putting up his personal assets to pay your bill. It is often effective when a wealthy person backs a new business. Be certain to obtain the guarantor's personal financial statement to ensure the guarantee is worth having. It is also good practice to acknowledge receipt of the guarantee formally with a letter sent certified mail — return receipt requested.

Not only can persons guarantee payment, corporations may guarantee the debts of other corporations, provided such a guarantee is not "ultra vires" or not contrary to the terms of their corporate charter. To protect yourself, request a resolution authorizing issuance of the guarantee signed by both the corporate secretary and the president. Always acknowledge the receipt of the guarantee formally with a certified letter.

It is also good practice to inform a guarantor of significant changes in credit exposure. While most guarantees will contain a waiver of this right, it makes good business sense to follow-up on it. The guarantor will then view the guarantee as an active working document that you intend to rely upon if things don't work out.

Another form of security, which is becoming quite popular, is the standby letter of credit. While irrevocable (non-cancellable) letters of credit have been used in export trade for many years, the standby is becoming more accepted in domestic use. The value of a standby letter of credit, however, is added to the customer's outstanding credit line by his bank. If your customer doesn't qualify for an adequate bank credit line, he probably won't be able to obtain the standby letter of credit.

A standby letter of credit works like this: Your customer applies to his bank for a document called a standby letter of credit. His bank makes the letter payable to you upon presentation of documents, usually your invoice, a sight draft and your statement that the customer has not paid within the payment terms you have previously agreed upon. Upon the receipt of valid documents, the bank will pay you.

The standby differs from a regular letter of credit because neither you nor your customer expect the bank to pay under normal circumstances. Payment occurs only if your customer doesn't pay as agreed. If you are forced to present your draft to the bank, the bank will take a dim view of the customer.

The primary advantage your customer will enjoy is that you are accepting his credit for your normal credit terms. This gives him an opportunity to build up a good payment history with you. He will find the standby less expensive than prepaying with borrowed money.

These are but three devices credit managers have used to reduce risk of loss from credit sales to marginal accounts. There are countless others involving assignment of passbook accounts, assignment of accounts receivable, inventory or equipment under the Uniform Commercial Code (UCC).

Before we leave marginal accounts, let me show you an easy method of monitoring these changeable accounts. It is called a *payment history* and a sample is shown on the next page. By completing this history each month you will be evaluating your marginal accounts on a regular basis. You can do this manually or by computer. The history can be as elaborate as you want to make it, but you should use a tool like this to stay on top of these accounts, which can significantly affect your performance.

You use the history as follows: At the end of each month, copy the balance owed by each customer from your receivable aging. This shows balances owed by aging categories, normally in five 30-day increments. For example, at January 31, January invoices would be shown current. If these same January invoices were unpaid at February 28, they would be shown as past due 1-30 days. You may also indicate unusual circumstances under "remarks" or even indicate collection efforts.

This history alerts you to customer payments becoming slower or exposures increasing, thus prompting you to take immediate and appropriate action.

Customer Payment History

Customer Name ______________ Account Number __________

Address ______________________ Credit Limit ______________

City/State/Zip ________________ Telephone ________________

Contact Name ________________ Title ____________________

DAYS PAST DUE

29

Month	Total	Current	1-30	31-60	61-90	90+	Remarks
Jan	234	234					
Feb	300	66	234				
Mar	300		66	234			
Apr	320	20		66	234		
May	330	10	20		66	234	
Jun	220		10	20		190	
Jul	150			10	20	120	
Aug							Charge off Bankrupt

Note: While this merely represents an aging of the account at the end of each month, and payments must be inferred, it presents a graphic picture, which is especially effective when discussing marginal accounts with sales people.

Some companies compute an imputed interest charge at the rate they consider their cost of capital. If it was 12% per year, in the example above (where the amounts are in thousands) multiply the past due by .01 for each month. For June, the amount would be $2,200. Some companies recap the charges for a year for each customer, then present the total lost by the company from slow payments to their sales people for them to use in negotiating prices with the customer for the coming year.

Chapter 4

Invoicing Effectively

The primary purpose of an invoice is to ask a customer to pay a bill. There is no other document that does this automatically. As a credit manager, you must therefore be certain this document does the job effectively for you. Do not let this vital document be distorted, changed or made less effective for the sake of your owner's ego (massive letterhead), your sales manager's attempt to perform marketing after the sale (distracting sales messages) or your controller's attempt to document costs, record inventory or track sales commission costs.

The primary purpose of your invoice is to ask your customer to pay his bill. Therefore your invoice must be:

- Simple and uncluttered.
- Carry only the information your customer needs to pay the bill.
- Effective enough to encourage your customer to pay the bill.
- Easy for your customer to process and pay.

It will make your job so much easier if you can start your collection with a clean, simple and effective document. But to change the existing invoice in most companies will require a strong personal selling job by the credit manager, for the owner, sales manager and controller will be attempting to make their jobs easier too. A compromise that often works is to print two sets of invoices with the one going to the customer containing considerably less information than the copy used internally.

Let's now discuss what essential elements your invoice must contain:

- It must clearly indicate that it is an invoice so place the word "invoice" prominently in the upper left hand corner. (This is where most people's eyes focus when they first look at a document.) Doing this will ensure that your invoice will be promptly directed to your customer's accounts payable section, not the traffic, sales or receiving departments.
- Your customer will want to make certain he owes the bill so indicate his correct legal name and billing address plus his order reference number (purchase order number or name of his employee ordering material or service) below the word "invoice."
- In the upper right hand corner, tell your customer who you are. Here is the place where your owner or sales manager can place his logo or letterhead, as long as it is not totally overpowering. Do not place an address here!
- You will want your customer to reference this document when he sends you a check so indicate your invoice number next. Avoid using letters since many accounts payable systems can accept only numbers. You will want your *complete* reference shown on the remittance advice of your customer's check for easy application of his payment.
- The invoice date should be shown next. Should the invoice date be different from the shipping date or work performed date? Use the earliest date on which your customer incurred the legal obligation to pay you. Using any other date not only confuses your customer, it will result in a payment delay if you happen to bill late.
- The terms of payments are next. Indicate terms your customer will understand, such as net 30 days or net on

receipt of invoice. I've seen terms of "net cash." What does that mean? Indicate the F.O.B. point if appropriate. This is the location where title of the goods passes to the customer. Unless otherwise indicated, the customer pays freight from this point.

- We then move to the body of the invoice. It is here that you record such identification as part number, product description, unit price, unit of measure, quantity shipped and extended amount. If your customer's purchase order uses a different name or number for your product, indicate his number or description also. This will make it easier for him to pay.
- At the bottom of the invoice, subtotal material or service, indicate freight as a separate item, indicate tax as a separate item, and indicate the exact amount of the cash discount you offer and the date payment must be received to earn it. (Note: If you allow the customer to calculate discount, he may make a mistake. So why take the chance?)
- Below these subtotals, print prominently:
Please Pay This Amount: $XXX.XX (inserting the amount) and list the address where you wish the customer to mail his check.
- In the lower left hand corner, indicate where your customer should direct his inquiries (if any). Include only the telephone number and perhaps the name of the person to contact. (Do not indicate an address as your customer may mail checks there).
- At the very bottom of the invoice indicate that the terms and conditions of sale are printed on the reverse side.

You can see that we have included a great deal of information on this document and that there is absolutely no room for extraneous detail. The invoice, however, contains all of the information the customer needs to pay the bill.

The time you take to make your invoice effective will pay great dividends later when you measure your collection results.

Now, examine your company's invoice. Does it contain all of these essential elements? If not, redesigning it should be given top priority.

When you have completed your design, pretend you are now an accounts payable supervisor. Could you process this invoice easily? You may wish to visit your company's accounts payable department and review the invoices they receive in a day. Ask the department supervisors what they think of your invoice. Your review will emphasize the matching process that goes on in most companies when they pay bills. A purchase order and a receiving document must match your invoice exactly if it is to be paid. If there are discrepancies between the documents, your customer will then set them aside for investigation and that could delay your payment.

One other important note. Why not use special envelopes for invoices clearly indicating that one is enclosed. That way, your customer's mail room can immediately route your invoice to the accounts payable department. In a large company, this could save a day or more.

By now, you're probably thinking: Am I going to do the billing too? No, but as a credit manager you should be vitally interested in how prompt and accurately it is done. Periodically, you should check shipping dates (from bills of lading) against the date your invoice is mailed. You should also analyze recurrent mistakes in billing and eliminate them. (Your customers will tell you about them when they pay, don't pay or short pay.)

Your job as a credit manager is to manage the cash inflows of your company. This includes direct or indirect management of all of the departments that impact cash inflows. Constant monitoring is an integral part of your job assignment as credit manager.

We're not done yet. Imagine yourself in a court room in front of a judge, attempting to collect money from a customer. How will you prove to the judge that your customer owes you money? How else but by reviewing your invoice and related documents such as the customer's purchase order, shipping documents, etc. Does your revised invoice support your collection case? Can any person looking at your invoice determine the balance due? This means your invoice should be a self-contained document, that is, it must stand on its own without any supporting documents.

Invoicing is an essential part of the collection process. Without an effective invoice, a credit manager is doomed from the start.

When considering invoicing, it is appropriate to discuss the role of lockboxes. A lockbox is a post office box rented by your bank to receive checks from your customers. Two or three times a day, the bank goes to this lockbox and deposits your customer's checks into your checking account. Then the bank sends you copies of the checks so you can post these amounts to your customer accounts receivable. In this way, your company receives benefit of the payments immediately.

Some companies still ask customers to mail checks to their office and deposit the checks only after they post the checks to the accounts receivable. The customers are quite happy with this procedure since it delays the charge to their bank account. Banks call this transit time between the date a check is written and the date a check clears the account "float." This delay, however, means cash is not immediately available to your company — cash your company may have to borrow.

As a credit manager, you must be concerned with the total cash inflows available to your company. Considering the effects of float will help you in forecasting collections. In addition, the sooner you deposit customer checks, the sooner you will be notified in the event they are returned for any reason by your customer's bank.

Invoice

Credit Risk Management Associates, Inc.

Sold To ______________________________

____

____

Customer Reference ______________________________

Invoice Number ______________

Invoice Date ______________

Terms of Payment ______________

Item No.	Item Description	Quantity	Item Price	Extension

Subtotal-Material ______________

Freight Amount ______________

Tax Amount ______________

Pay This Amount ______________

Direct Questions To ______________________________

Telephone ______________________________

Mail Check To ______________________________

Lockbox Address ______________________________

Subject to Terms and Conditions on the Reverse Side

____

Chapter 5

Collecting Past Due Accounts

Once we've approved a customer for credit acceptance, billed the invoice and waited for the invoice to become due, the collection process begins. Remember, stage one of the collection process is the invoice — the document requesting payment. If the invoice is correct and the customer is able and willing to pay, a check should be received in your lockbox on the due date. If it isn't received, there is a problem.

When companies derive the price of their products and services, they assume customer payments will meet their credit sales terms. Whenever payment is not received on time, this profit erosion, in effect, gives the customer an involuntary price discount.

Immediately upon learning that an account is past due, the credit manager must review the account in terms of:

1. The *amount* of the invoice. How crucial is the payment to your company?
2. The *age* of the past due. Is it possible the customer has merely grouped invoices for fewer payments per month?
3. The *credit risk* of the customer. Did you anticipate slow payment and if so, what precautionary steps have you taken? (see Chapter 3.)

After this review, most credit managers set up a collection file for the customer, which includes the following information:

1. Legal name of the customer, billing address, telephone number, and name and title of the collection contact. (Information we obtained previously when the account was establshed.)
2. Amount past due and an itemization of the individual transactions comprising the balance owing.
3. The results of past collection contacts and the past payment history of the customer. (Information from your payment history.)

With this information, the credit manager can select the appropriate collection approach.

When attempting to collect a large number of accounts, it is often helpful to classify past due customers in several categories. (The risk categories are taken from Chapter 1.)

1. For A and B credit risks who have paid promptly in the past and who have given no indication that the problem is anything more serious than a misplaced invoice, a statement or past due notice is usually sufficient.
2. For D credit risks where slow payment is normal, a decision must be made whether they should be contacted by statement or telephone.
3. For D credit risks where payment is slower than normal, the credit file is reviewed and updated before a telephone call is made.
4. For E credit risks, because of their unusual nature, a special discussion with internal management is usually required. In these discussions the decisions leading up to initial approval are reviewed and special approaches to be used to handle the account are considered.

If the account has just become past due, unless the amount is significantly large, most credit managers will assume the customer wants to pay but has overlooked the invoice and needs a gentle friendly reminder. A past due statement or form collection letter is used.

Ten working days later, if payment has not been received, the collection process enters the "what is wrong" stage. At this point, the credit manager still assumes the customer wants to pay but that an existing problem prevents him from doing so. The first step is to make sure everything is in order. Invoices and delivery tickets supporting the transaction are reviewed. A call is made to the sales and customer service departments to make certain a credit memo or adjustment isn't in process.

Only after these conditions are fulfilled is personal contact made by the credit manager. He still assumes the customer wants to pay but he must find out for certain if that is actually the case, and if the customer is still able to pay. A collection telephone call may go something like this:

> "Is this Mr. Jones of ABC Company? This is Rusty Rutherford of CRMA and I'm calling about your past due account." (Pause twenty seconds . . . this gives the customer an opportunity to respond.) Most questions should be open-ended and the credit manager must let the customer talk as much as possible and restrain from attempting to dominate the conversation. It's better to simply provide subtle direction to the call, to keep the call on track about getting payment now.
>
> "My account's past due? I'm certain we mailed you a check just last week. My company always pays its bills."
>
> "Mr. Jones, I'm sure that that's the case. Could you give me your check number, check date, and the amount of the check so I can trace your payment or should I contact your bookkeeper?"
>
> "She isn't in today. But I'll check with her first thing."
>
> "Mr. Jones, it's important we get this cleared right away. Couldn't you check for me, please?"
>
> "Why don't you call me tomorrow morning?"
>
> "Thank you for taking time to talk to me, Mr. Jones. I'll call you at 9 a.m. tomorrow. Good bye."

Notice that the credit manager continued the conversation until he received a definite commitment. If the customer defers again the next day, it is probably time to get the salesman involved. (Salesmen are too valuable to perform *routine* collections. They should become involved only when asked by the credit manager or when personal contact is essential.)

A good collector contacts the customer until he receives an unconditional commitment to pay a specific amount by a specific date. If the customer gives this commitment, the credit manager repeats it using terms the customer can visualize such as: "Then you will mail me a check for $4,567.89 tomorrow morning to bring your account up to date."

This is much better than: "Please send the amount due soon."

The most effective collection technique is a personal customer visit. Next best is the telephone, for it provides immediate feedback as to the customer's intention to pay. Problem collection calls should always be confirmed by letter, especially if the repayment arrangements are complex or involve payments to be made in more than a week.

The next best collection technique is the form collection letter. It can be used to gain total collection coverage with past due customers — the more personalized the better. All letters sent under your signature should be personally signed by you. Each collection letter must contain enough information so the customer knows what he has to pay. If a customer requires purchase order numbers, they should be included in the letter.

Some companies send a duplicate copy of an invoice with a sticker saying "Past due. Please remit." This is cold and the word "remit" is insensitive. A more effective approach would be to send a duplicate copy of the invoice with a handwritten note by the credit manager, including his signature and telephone number.

Finally, when faced with a large number of accounts, the credit manager may use computer generated past-due notices. These notices must contain all the information the customer needs to pay his bill and must indicate that his account has exceeded the terms of payment agreed to when his credit was accepted.

Our collection program has now gone through two stages:

1. Invoice.
2. Friendly reminder.

There is also a third stage and it's called the "what is wrong" stage. Here, the credit manager must make contact with the customer himself, or call in the salesman for help. The purpose is to determine whether our company should continue to solicit the customer's business or to discontinue sales and get the money owed using appropriate legal remedies.

This decision can best be made by a face to face discussion with the customer. It makes no difference whether a salesman or credit manager conducts the customer interview. Both should be present, for, after the meeting, our company will decide whether to keep this firm as a customer or classify it as a debtor.

If these three collection contacts have failed, the credit manager changes his attitude toward the customer. Up through stage three, the credit manager has assumed the customer wants to pay. If the customer is not willing to make a satisfactory commitment by stage three, the collection process moves into stage four.

In this stage, the credit manager is now concerned that the customer may not want to pay or is financially unable to pay. In the credit manager's eyes, the customer has turned into a debtor. This is another way of saying that it's now more important to get the money than to retain the customer's good will. This stage is normally handled by letter and is called the *moral obligation stage.* A sample moral obligation letter follows this chapter.

The strategy in this stage is to remind the debtor of his moral obligation to keep a promise, a promise he made when your company accepted his credit. Avoid making the mistake of reminding the debtor that non-payment will endanger his credit record. This is a threat and quite a weak argument. Stick to his personal moral obligation to your company when he applied for credit by signing your credit application and the obligation your company expects all its customers to keep.

Finally, if no answer or check is received from the customer, the collection moves into the fifth and final stage — *you have a legal obligation to pay us*. The United States operates under both State and Federal laws. These laws give businessmen the legal right to collect debts owed by another through legal process in a court of competent jurisdiction. This final demand letter must be carefully worded so as not to constitute a threat. This statement of action is sent when payment is not made by a certain date. A sample letter follows this chapter.

The secret to good collection practice is organization and systematic follow-up of debtor promises. The credit manager who is consistent in his follow-up will have better than average success.

COLLECTIONS BY THIRD PARTIES

After the final demand letter has been written advising that a third party will enter into the collection process if payment is not made, the credit manager should not procrastinate in referring the account to a collection attorney or agency. Otherwise, his final demand letter is a threat which can often violate State collection laws. The file referring to the third party should contain:

1. A statement of the account and copies of documents supporting the statement.
2. A copy of any collection correspondence from the debtor and those written by the credit manager.
3. A copy of the business credit application and a copy of the debtor's check.

You have the option to send a copy of the credit report if such practice is not prohibited by the reporting agency.

Some credit managers feel they have failed if they turn an account over to an agency. They may even make it difficult for the agency to collect by unconsciously failing to include important documents describing disputes or collections.

Sending an account to an agency or attorney is simply another way of bringing in the cash. If the collection agency succeeds where a credit manager has failed, that should only be evidence that the agency has done a good job, and the credit manager should be complimented for having found a way to collect the bill.

Collection Record

Customer Name ______________________________

Customer Telephone __________ Collection Contact __________

Credit Risk ________ Limit ________ Past Payment Record ____

Date	By	Spoke To	Results	Follow-up Date

Moral Obligation Letter

Jones Oil Company
123 South Gusher Drive
Houston, TX 77001

Balance Due $4,567.89

Dear Mr. Jones:

We have attempted to contact you several times regarding the past due status of your account with Credit Risk Management Associates, Inc. This balance of $4567.89 dates from February and is seriously past due.

44 Our company accepted your credit in good faith under our standard terms of net 30 days and we expected payment promptly as we do from all of our customers. You have accepted our product but haven't given us any explanation of why payment is being withheld.

Unfortunately, your continued silence will force us to consider more serious handling of the collection.

We are confident you will keep your promise by sending us a check for $4567.89 or an explanation today.

Sincerely yours,

Rusty Rutherford
Credit Manager

Legal Obligation Letter

Jones Oil Company
123 South Gusher Drive
Houston, TX 77001

Balance Due: $4567.89

Dear Mr. Jones:

There comes a time — an urgent time — in the collection of a past due account when it seems there is no alternative but to refer handling to a third party for appropriate legal action. This appears to apply to your account.

We have attempted to contact you on numerous occasions without success but, as of today, have not received your check nor any explanation of why you have not paid this legitimate billing.

Unfortunately, unless your check is received by 8 a.m., Thursday, November 6, 19XX at my office at 123 5th Street, Houston, TX 77001, I shall refer handling to our collection agent, the Houston Association of Credit Management.

Collection agencies will collect. Otherwise, they earn no fee. They will take whatever action is necessary including the employment of attorneys to take appropriate legal action.

We sincerely hope this serious action does not become necessary.

This is final!

Yours very truly,

Rusty Rutherford
Credit Manager

45

Chapter 6

Handling Disputes and Complaints

Disputes and complaints are largely ignored by most textbooks on credit. Yet many credit managers say resolving customer disputes and complaints often takes up 35 to 40 percent of time. In this section, we'll cover some of the "tricks of the trade" for these disciplines.

Some people say that resolving customer complaints and disputes is not the responsibility of the credit manager. While the credit manager can do very little himself to directly resolve these problems, nonetheless, unless he takes an active role to encourage others to resolve them, they remain on his accounts receivable indefinitely.

We will be using the term *exception receivable* to describe any invoice a customer refuses to pay because he feels it is an incorrect bill. Some authorities state that exception receivables can often represent 20 percent or more of the average credit manager's receivable portfolio. By resolving these items quickly you will be removing a negative reflection on your performance.

Let's point out quickly that the initial responsibility of the credit manager is to determine whether a customer complaint is really a legitimate dispute or whether the customer is masking a collection problem, such as not having the money to pay. A quick way of doing this is to use the following strategy:

- Get the customer to define the problem in terms that can be dealt with. (Don't accept the allegation, "Your company screwed up." Determine exactly what was wrong.)

- Get the customer to propose a solution. (This will force the customer to define the problem more precisely in dollars and cents — terms that can be dealt with. For example, "I either want you to send me another widget at no charge or credit my account with you.")
- Get the customer to pay what is owed. (If the customer requests a $200 credit on a $1000 invoice, he should pay the $800 he does not dispute. If he won't, you, as credit manager, have a collection problem, not an exception receivable.)

The reason exception receivables are time-consuming is that their resolution often crosses many department lines. Typically, the sales department must investigate the customer's request for adjustment, prepare a *request for credit memo,* send the request through several layers of sales management for approval, then obtain the controller's concurrence. This takes time, for these top people are often very busy.

Even in the case of a simple return of damaged product, the manufacturing plant must prepare a *returned goods report,* send it to the sales department, obtain final approval from the financial department and then post it to the customer's account receivable.

Besides the complicated and time-consuming approval process, there is no incentive either to the sales or manufacturing departments to issue a credit memo, for in the case of the sales department, it means a negative sale or reduction of revenue or, in the case of the manufacturing department, an increased expense (if the returned product must be scrapped) or an increased inventory (if the product must be returned to stock).

Only if your company is truly customer-oriented and cares about the implications of customer dissatisfaction and irritation will the credit memo process be a smooth and quick one. It is so easy to hide these exception receivables until auditors go through the books at year end.

Clearly, your job as a credit manager is to report these exception receivables monthly so they won't become a surprise at year end. The first step is to implement an exception receivable reporting system, if one is not in force now. A sample form to use is shown at the end of this chapter. The *exception receivable report,* or ERR for short, has four objectives:

1. It reports the problem to management. (A copy of each report should be sent to the controller and sales manager to alert them to possible reductions in sales.)
2. It defines the problem reported by the customer concisely and offers the customer's proposed solution to the problem.
3. It assigns responsibility for resolution of the problem to a particular individual, thus forcing that individual to act.
4. It assigns a target date for completion. (People seem to get things done when assigned a completion date.)

The preparation of this report is the responsibility of the credit manager and he should recap outstanding ERRs and their dollar impact each month in a report to the sales, manufacturing and financial managers.

Because most customer requests for adjustment result in a credit memo issued against their account receivable, some companies, upon receiving the complaint from the customer, deduct the amount in question from the customer's account receivable and charge it to the sales department as expense. This forces the sales department to either accept the charge or re-invoice the customer.

Let's discuss in some detail those rare situations where your company cannot acceed to a customer's request for adjustment. The first step for you, the credit manager, is to obtain, in writing, a clear statement of your company's position. Then, you will probably have to relay this disappointing decision to the customer. Do so by letter.

Your letter should be comprised of four parts:

1. Tell the customer that you are glad he brought the problem to your attention and that your company fully investigated his request.

2. Allow the customer to save face (if possible) by apologizing for the misunderstanding.
3. Sell the customer on the reasonableness of the solution.
4. Ask the customer to pay what is owed.

With this letter include an invoice for the amount in dispute so the customer will have a document from which to pay the amount owed.

If the time from receipt of complaint to decision is relatively short, your company will minimize customer irritation and keep uncollectable balances in your receivable aging to a minimum.

To summarize, the responsibility of a credit manager in dealing with exception receivables is to gather the facts from the customer and/or field sales representative, obtain the customer's proposed solution to present to management, collect the amount not in dispute, follow-up to obtain a management decision and convey the final decision to the customer. While handling of these ERR's is troublesome, the reputation of the credit department can be affected by how these customer contacts are handled. With proper handling, the credit manager may reduce receivable investment significantly.

Exception Receivable Report

To: Sales Manager

Date: December 1, 19XX

From: Credit Manager

Re: Harold J. Smith and Sons Inc. Houston, Texas	Disputed Amount: Our Invoice No:	$432.23 23456

PROBLEM: On December 1, 19XX, Harold Smith, telephoned me stating that the price on our shipment of 14 valves was not that quoted to him by our sales person, Jeannette Jones. Jeannette said that a quantity discount of 10% would be offered if Smith ordered 10 or more. Smith requests that a credit memo be issued for $432.23. He agrees to pay the remaining balance due on the account.

Target Date For Resolution: December 15, 19XX

Chapter 7

Basics of Receivable Accounting

Some credit managers feel that since they are not accountants they should not be required to perform accounting work. This is not realistic. Most credit managers report to a controller and his work involves analysis by numerical methods. This means a credit manager must report his performance monthly in numerical terms (see Chapter 10) and must frequently interface with accountants. If the credit manager doesn't understand basic bookkeeping and fundamental accounting, he may often be led astray. This chapter, then, will introduce basic entries affecting receivables and some of the terminology used by our close friends in accounting.

The majority of businesses use a method of double entry booking, which means that each accounting entry has two sides or parts: a *debit* and a *credit. In an asset account such as receivables, a debit entry increases the asset while a credit entry reduces it.* For example, if a customer pays us $100 on his account, we debit cash, and credit or reduce receivables. If that same customer's check is returned NSF by the bank for non sufficient funds, we credit cash, and debit or increase receivables.

In a liability account, just the opposite occurs, a credit entry increases accounts payable while a debt decreases accounts payable.

When we have entries affecting the profit and loss accounts such as sales or expenses, the expense entries act like asset accounts and the sales entries act the opposite. For example, if we make a sale of $100 on a credit basis, we debit receivables and credit sales. If we write off a receivable as a bad debt, we credit receivables and debit expense. If we issue a credit memo to a customer's account, we credit receivables and debit or reduce sales. Note: It will be extremely helpful to you if you always think of the receivable entry first. Remember, *a debit increases receivables and a credit reduces receivables.*

Now, what is the entry for a cash sale? You increased an asset, cash, so you debit cash and credit sales. Not so hard after all!

Many companies do not write off receivables directly to *bad-debt expense.* Instead, they set up an *allowance for bad debts* at the beginning of the year and add equal amounts to this allowance each month, usually, a percentage of sales that equals their prior year experience. What accounting entry will you use to set up an allowance for bad debts? Debit bad-debt expense and credit the allowance for bad debts. Then, when we write off a receivable, we credit receivables and debit the allowance for bad debts. How simple this is, yet countless hours are spent arguing about these simple entries.

Remember our discussion in the previous chapter about the reason sales departments dislike issuing credit memos. The accounting impact of a credit memo is to credit receivables and debit (reduce) sales.

Accountants like to refer to T-accounts. This is simply a short hand to show the effect of transactions on various accounts. For example, let's follow the receivable T-account through several transactions. First, we will make a credit sale for $100, issue a credit memo for $50, receive a customer payment of $25 and finally, write off $25 to bad debts. The T-accounts look like this:

Cash		Receivables		Sales		Expense	
25		100	50	50	100	25	
			25				
			25				

That was so easy, you probably want to make T-account entries for all of the transactions we discussed in this chapter.

Chapter 8

Introduction to Financial Statements

Most people are totally buffaloed by the term financial statements, and credit managers are not any different. But financials are not difficult once the basic rules (or conventions as accountants call them) are understood. Before going into the basics, I recommend you first read all the footnotes in any financial statement carefully. If there is anything unusual about the statement, this is where you will find it out.

Let's start with the *balance sheet.* This is a snapshot of a business at one point in time, such as December 31, 19XX. On the left hand side are *assets,* or things the business owns. Examples are cash in bank, inventory, furniture, building, land and, of course, receivables. On the right hand side are what the business owes to its bank, its suppliers, and to its stockholders or owners, called *liabilities* and *equity.*

Starting with *assets,* each category or line item is listed in order of liquidity, that is, how quickly it can be turned into cash. *Cash in bank or cash on hand* is totally liquid so it is listed first. Next comes *marketable securities* or stock that can be sold and turned into cash. *Receivables,* amounts owed to the company by its customers, can be turned into cash if collected by an effective credit manager. *Inventory* is listed next, for once the goods are sold, they are turned into cash. All of these items are normally turned into cash one year from the date of the balance sheet so they are called *current assets.*

In addition to current assets are *fixed assets,* assets the business does not normally turn into cash unless it is going out of business or is experiencing extremely tough times. Land, airplanes, furniture and fixtures are examples.

Now to *liabilities,* or what the business owes. These are listed on the right side of the balance sheet in the order in which they are normally paid. First, normally are *payables,* amounts due to trade suppliers, usually in 30 days. Next come *short-term bank loans,* payable to the bank within one year. If a business has bank loans due in say, five years, the amount due the first year is shown as *current portion of long-term debt* and the amount due the remaining four years is shown as *long-term liabilities.*

Next are *accruals* or estimates of charges that will be paid within a year. Examples are accruals for taxes payable or payroll. All bills to be paid within one year from the balance sheet date are subtotaled as *current liabilities.*

Long-term liabilities come next. These would include the last four years of the five-year bank loan we mentioned earlier, and subordinated debentures or any other long-term debt. Finally, we come to the *equity* section — the amounts owed to the stockholders or the owners. If we add up the assets or wealth of the business, then subtract what the business owes to outsiders, we arrive at *equity,* also called *net worth.*

Equity (net worth) consists of three parts. First, we list the par value of the stock called *capital* that is issued and outstanding. This is merely an accounting convention or rule. Next, we list *paid-in capital,* or the amount paid for the stock in excess of the par value. For convenience, we will call both of these capital. The next part is *retained earnings,* sometimes called by the old fashioned title of surplus. It represents the profits of the business which have not been paid out as dividends or rewards to the stockholders. And it's a running score since the business began. You can see that if there were losses, these would be subtracted from the earlier profits.

Now we know enough to construct a simple balance sheet:

Balance Sheet

December 31, 19X3

Assets	*Liabilities*
Current Assets	**Current Liabilities**
Cash on hand and in bank	Payables
Marketable securities	Bank loan payable
Receivables	Current portion of long-term debt
Inventory	Accruals
Fixed Assets	**Long-Term Liabilities**
Land	Long-term debt
Fixtures	
Building	
	Equity (net worth)
	Capital stock
	Retained earnings
Total Assets	**Total Liabilities and Equity**

Admittedly, this is a very simple balance sheet. But it does balance and we have discussed the idea of liquidity. Remember, assets we expect to turn into cash within one year from the balance sheet date are listed as current assets, and bills we must pay within one year are current liabilities. If you take current assets and subtract current liabilities, what do you have? In effect, you have the margin of safety in liquidity. Accountants call this *working capital.* What if current liabilities are larger than current assets? Obviously, the business will probably not be able to pay its bills. We call this *negative working capital* and it is sure a sign of concern.

Let us now turn our attention to the *profit and loss statement.*

Unlike the balance sheet, which we said can be compared to a snapshot, the profit and loss statement can be compared to a movie, for it has a beginning and an end.

The first item is *sales;* some people call it revenue. This is the gross amount sold by the business in the period of time covered by the P&L statement. Next we have to deduct what it cost us to make the product. This is called *cost of goods sold.* To find this amount, we take the *inventory* at the beginning of the period, add *purchases* during the period, and subtract the *ending inventory.*

Next we subtract other expenses associated with the production of the product called *operating expenses.* If we subtract cost of goods sold and operating expenses from sales, we have *gross profit.*

Credit managers and salesmen have to be paid, so we next subtract *non-operating expenses* sometimes called burden. This brings us to *net profit before tax.* Next we subtract *tax* and obtain *profit after tax,* often called simply PAT. This is the bottom line. The amount on this line, after paying dividends is transferred to the retained earnings on the balance sheet.

Our profit and loss statement will look like this:

Profit and Loss Statement

January 1, 19X3 to December 31, 19X3

Sales		________
Beginning inventory	________	
Plus: Purchases	________	
Subtotal	________	
Less: Ending inventory	________	
Cost of goods sold	________	
Less: Cost of goods sold		________
Gross margin		
Less: Operating expenses		________
Gross profit		
Less: Non-operating expenses		________
Net profit before tax		
Less: Taxes		________
Net profit after tax (to balance sheet)		________

Just to see if you are alert, what item appears as the same line item on both the balance sheet and the profit and loss statement?

Most credit managers don't analyze financial statements in excruciating detail. It is usually because we don't have the time or the lines of credit requested aren't that substantial. But there are some basic ratios most of us compute routinely to determine quickly whether it is probable the customer will pay his bills.

Here are six ratios I use. We'll define each and then tell you what they mean:

Liquid Ratio. This is also called the acid test, or quick ratio. It is calculated by adding cash and receivables and dividing the result into current liabilities. This ratio will tell you if the customer can pay current liabilities out of cash and receivables only. It is best if this ratio is at least .8:1. Another way of saying this is that the business can pay 80% of its current liabilities out of its most liquid assets.

Current Ratio. This ratio is computed by dividing current assets by current liabilities. It used to be an old rule of thumb that this ratio had to be at least 2:1. In today's environment, 1:1 is usually satisfactory.

Receivable Turn. Divide the sales by the number of days in the period covered by the profit and loss statement. This result is called sales per day. Now divide receivables by sales per day and multiply the result by 30. If the result is more than 30, the company is not turning its receivables into cash within 30 days and may pay you slower than 30 days (the normal terms of trade in most industries).

Inventory Turn. Divide the cost of goods sold (CGS) by the number of days in the period covered by the profit and loss statement. This is called CGS per day. Divide inventory by CGS per day and multiply the result by 30. You can see that if inventory turn is 30 and receivable turn is 30, it apparently is taking your customer 60 days on average to take his purchases from you and turn them into cash he can use to pay you. Of course, life is not this simple, but the ratios can give you a feel for anticipated payments. Comment: We use cost of goods sold for inventory turn rather than sales because we want to compare apples to apples. Our inventory figure doesn't have profit built-in while sales does. Of course, if the sales figure is all you have, use it.

Payables Turn. Divide payables by CGS per day and multiply the result by 30. This will tell you how many days of purchases are unpaid.

Debt To Equity. This ratio will tell you how many dollars the customer has invested in his business and how many dollars the creditors have invested in the customer's business. Simply divide total liabilities by equity. If you have the time, you may wish to compare the ratios you have computed for your customer's business with industry averages or those of similar customers.

This concludes our brief investigation of a single financial statement. What if you have the fortune to obtain balance sheets for two dates? Then you can perform comparative analysis! Sounds exciting. Stay with me.

One of the most useful techniques a credit manager can use is to develop a source and use of funds statement. This will tell what funds came into the business and how they were used.

Funds can come from three sources:

1. A liability can increase. A bank loan increases. Trade suppliers accept more of the business's credit.
2. Equity can increase. The owners can put more money into the business or the business can make profits and keep them in the company.
3. An asset can be decreased. If receivables are collected and the amount tied up in receivables is less, funds will be available for use elsewhere.

On the opposite hand, funds can be used in three ways:

1. A liability can decrease. The bank can demand repayment of its loan. Suppliers can refuse to accept the company's credit and sell C.O.D. (cash on delivery).
2. Equity can decrease. The business can lose money and reduce its retained earnings. The owners can take money out of the business.
3. An asset can increase. This will tie up funds that can't be used for anything else.

Let's try an example.

Balance Sheet December 19X3		Balance Sheet December 19X4		Source	Use
Cash	$ 400	Cash	$ 400	—	—
Receivables	500	Receivables	1500	—	$1000
Inventory	1000	Inventory	500	$ 500	—
Fixed assets	2000	Fixed assets	1000	1000	—
Payables	600	Payables	1000	400	—
Bank	3000	Bank	500	—	2500
Equity	300	Equity	1900	1600	—
				$3500	$3500

Now, what does all this tell us?

Funds came from four sources. The business made $1600 or the owners invested an additional $1600 in the firm. Suppliers accepted $400 more of the company's credit, $1000 in fixed assets were sold and inventory was reduced by $500. These funds were used to pay off the bank by $1500 and to accept an additional credit from the company's customers. The $10 million question is: Will you be paid better as a result? I think you will.

Take a deep breath! We're through, almost. I've said credit managers usually don't do in-depth analysis. But, if you are going to be a good credit manager, you should take the time to learn all you can about financials. The infrequent times you will need to analyze the financials will be your major credit exposures and, if you predict wrong, you stand to lose not only your credibility but perhaps your job.

We'll close by saying a word about the different types of financial statements. The best is a fiscal year-end statement since all adjustments are made to the books, especially the ending inventory. Most businesses take a physical inventory at this time and write off or expense shortages or losses from inventory. Remember I said the ending inventory appears in both the balance sheet and P&L statement.

It is also a better statement if it is prepared by a Certified Public Accountant and contains an unqualified opinion that the statement was prepared according to Generally Accepted Accounting Principles (GAAP). This should give you confidence that the figures accurately reflect the business and that no radical changes in accounting procedure were made. It also doesn't hurt to have the owner sign the statement to show he feels the figures are representative. If he won't sign, its a good idea to find out why.

Just in case you had trouble with the ratios, I'll summarize the formulas:

1. Liquid Ratio	Cash + Receivables	divided by	Current Liabilities
2. Current Ratio	Current Assets	divided by	Current Liabilities
3. Receivable Turn	Receivables	divided by	Sales per Day Times 30
4. Inventory Turn	Inventory	divided by	CGS per Day Times 30
5. Payables Turn	Payables	divided by	CGS per Day Times 30

Chapter 9

Using Computers in Credit Management

A credit manager is an information gatherer, a predictor, a motivator and a decision maker. To perform these functions effectively, information about customers must be obtained, stored, accessed or retrieved quickly, and presented effectively. Some people call our modern office a "symbol factory" because office people have had to develop codes to help them process the enormous amount of information their workload entailed.

Processing paperwork can often consume many credit departments, trapping the credit manager in the office thus restricting his visits to customers, which are such a vital part of his job. Any method we can use to reduce or process paperwork more effectively will certainly have a significant benefit to the average credit manager. This then, the control of data or information, is the subject of this chapter.

A credit manager works with several *information sources.* These sources supply information automatically or upon request.

The onslaught of paper is astounding. Credit applications, credit reports, salesman's call reports, sales order forms, invoice copies, statements, accounts receivable agings and requests for credit information are just some of the types of documents a credit department receives every day. Time management people tell us the truly organized person handles each piece of paper once, and only once. Won't it be great if we could achieve this goal?

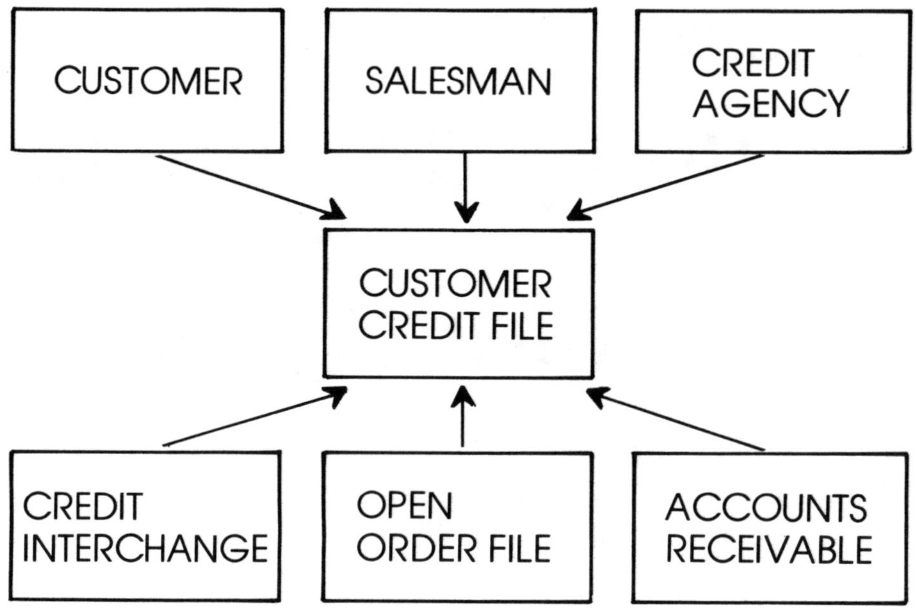

Following is a description of a credit system that I installed in two companies and has been in place for over four years. It certainly is not the ultimate system but elements might be appropriate for your department in your quest to reduce the time you spend handling paperwork.

Both of these credit departments were characterized by three elements:

- A large number of new customers with fairly low individual credit exposures.
- Demand for immediate credit approvals, usually within twenty minutes of the request.
- A limited amount of credit personnel.

Our goal was prompt turnaround of requests for credit approval of new customers. The "Credit Investigation Worksheet" (shown in Chapter 1) provided a means of recording the credit investigation from start to finish on one piece of paper. Investigations followed the flow chart shown on next page:

Request for approval by telephone

Prepare New Customer Credit Investigation Worksheet (NCCIW)

Look up customer in D&B Reference Book to verify name.

Check to see that no credit file exists.

Order D&B Report using computer terminal

Order Credit Interchange Report using computer terminal

Telephone trade references and/or bank recording on NCCIW

Review industry publications for volume data, licenses

Analyze data. Contact sales department if necessary or customer

Determine appropriate risk code, credit limit and approved payment terms. Add codes on NCCIW

Telephone approval to field office

Key codes into Customer Credit Control File

Once the information was keyed or typed into the computer file, the New Customer Credit Investigation Worksheet and computer printed credit reports were sent to a microfiche company for filming.

Does this sound too good to be true? Let us describe some of the elements of the system in more detail.

Here is a detailed description of the Customer Credit Control File. While your computer wizard or *programmer* must write the instructions to the computer, you, as a *user,* must define your file and tell the programmer what reports you wish and what you wish displayed on the computer screen.

Customer Credit Control File

Field Name	Size	Remarks
Credit Control Number	10	
Customer Legal Name	25	
Trade Style	25	
Cross Reference Name	25	
Address Line 1	25	
Address Line 2	25	
City	15	
State	2	
Zip Code	9	
Telephone	10	
Credit Limit	4	in thousands
Credit Risk Code	1	
Approved Payment Terms Code	1	
Date of Credit Approval	6	
Credit Approved By	15	
D-U-N-S Number	10	
D & B Rating	3	
D & B Report Date	6	
Interchange Report Number	10	
Interchange Rating	3	
Interchange Report Date	6	
SIC Code	4	
Date Business Started	4	
Legal Organization Code	1	
President or Owner's Name	25	
Date Our Account Opened	4	
Date of Last Sale	6	
Date of Last Payment	6	
Year-to-Date Sales	9	
High Credit Last 3 Months	9	
Owes Now	9	
Past Due	9	
Past Due Over 30 Days	9	
Past Due Over 90 Days	9	
Date of Oldest Item	6	
Weighted Average Days to Pay	3	
Responsible Salesperson	15	

Some of the names of the fields may be new to you. *Trade Style* is a name used by a business different from that of the legal entity responsible for payment. Often your sales people will know the customer as KATY while the legal name is Kartooom, Atchison, Topeka and Yamaha Feed Store Inc. *D-U-N-S Number* is a number used to identify a business organization assigned by Dun and Bradstreet. By having this number in your file, you can facilitate repeat inquiries to the D&B computer file. *SIC Code* is a four digit number assigned to an industry by the Federal government. D&B includes this number assigned to a business in their *Reference Book* and in their Business Information Report on a particular business. *Weighted Average Days to Pay* is a calculation of the average days it took your customer to pay each invoice weighted by the size of each.

Once you have defined your file to your programmer, you must design the reports you wish. For example, your sales department might like a list of all of the customers that have been approved for credit and what their outstanding balances are. In this system, a report called a *Field Manager's Credit Guide* is published monthly for the use of all sales people. Below is an example:

Field Manager's Credit Guide

CUSTOMER	RISK CODE	LIMIT	OWES	PAST DUE	LAST SALE
Allright Co	B	$500	$ 50	$ 25	10-20-8X
Bobco Inc	E	10	1	1	3-10-8X
David's Drums	D	50	25	25	9-15-8X
Jerry Limited	A	$999	14	6	11-01-8X

Suppose that a new sales person was recently hired and you wanted to furnish her with a list of only her customers, their assigned credit limits, risk codes and payment terms. Using the computer, the list can usually be compiled in minutes.

You can probably think of many useful reports: Accounts Exceeding Credit Limits; Out of Date Credit Reports; Listing of Past Due Amounts in Descending Order, Credit Risk Complexion of Sales, and on and on. Once you enter the information into the computer, the reports you can develop are endless if your files are well designed. In fact, credit managers with effective data processing often have the problem of too much information, not too little.

With the introduction of personal computers, credit managers have been given an opportunity to reduce clerical tasks to an absolute minimum. It behooves all progressive credit managers to make maximum use of their data processing resources.

A part of our "paperless" credit department is credit files on microfiche. The system works like this: Each piece of paper for microfiche is coded in the upper right hand corner with four pieces of information:

1. Credit Control Number
2. Type of Document
3. Document Date
4. Rating

The microfiche company then keys or types this information into their computer which automatically assigns a fiche location to the document. This information is presented in an index as shown below:

Microfiche Index

Number	Customer	Date	Type Document	Rating	Location
19-999	CRMA Inc	4-09-8X	D&B RPT	LNR	01 AA
12-567	Evelyn Inc	6-12-8X	D&B RPT	5A1	25 FF
11-978	Rogercat	5-22-8X	NCCIW	B10	03 DG
34-789	Susan LTD	3-11-8X	NACM RPT	AB4	15 DC

As a result, credit files on over 1200 customers appear on 70 microfiche cards which fit into pockets of five pages of an 8½ x 11 inch notebook. This eliminates use of 10 file cabinets.

Is microfiche expensive? Relatively not. About 15 cents per transaction. This is a great deal less than paying a filing clerk, and the time saved in looking up information and possibly duplicating misfiled information makes the system pay for itself in a very short time.

How else can a credit manager use the computer? In addition to word processing, one new application we are exploring at Weatherford is the use of MCI mail. Using IBM personal computers located in the credit department, we can enter letters to customers which are transmitted electronically to the nearest MCI regional center, printed with a laser printer with our letterhead and individual collector signature, and mailed to the customer usually within two days. If the customer has an MCI address, we can send him a message direct to his personal computer at even less cost than a letter. Hopefully, all of our larger customer accounts payable departments will allow us to communicate with them in this way.

One of the most frequent complaints from credit managers is that they simply don't have enough time to get done all the things they feel ought to be done. Using the computer to perform the routine tasks of information processing can free up more time than most of us can possibly imagine. Additionally, if the reports requested of the computer are only an exception action type, that is, they point out what needs to be done by highlighting only the items that require attention, use of the computer will allow us to concentrate on the important few rather than the trivial many.

Chapter 10

Evaluating Credit Performance

How do you evaluate a credit manager? This nagging questions can best be answered by examining the reasons a company establishes a credit department:

1. To avoid surprises from bad-debt losses by determining in advance the apparent or potential credit risk of the customer.
2. To ensure payment from high-risk accounts. (See Chapter 2.)
3. To collect past-due balances in a professional manner (preserving goodwill, while motivating the customer to pay his past-due bill).
4. To accurately predict the cash-in flows from credit sales.
5. To assist in handling customer complaints and disputes.
6. To alert management to changes in receivable trends within the company, the industry and among major customers, and to promptly report significant risks that exist or appear imminent.

With these major objectives as a start, let us look at some numerical measures of credit performance.

The first we will consider is *collection percentage*. This is, in my opinion, the best numerical measure. It is calculated by dividing collections received during the month by receivables outstanding at the beginning of the same month. A constantly increasing percentage indicates that cash is being collected sooner and should reflect a lower investment in receivables as compared to sales volume. This measure can be easily understood by management.

Next, the most popular measure: days sales outstanding or DSO. It is calculated in three steps:

1. Determine sales per day. Take sales for the period (year, quarter, month) and divide by the number of days in the period to find sales per day.
2. Divide receivables outstanding at the end of the period by sales per day.
3. Multiply the result by your normal terms of sale, usually 30 days.

While DSO can reflect lower receivable investment if it is presented over several periods of time, this numerical measure can be affected substantially by increasing or decreasing sales. For example, if sales are increasing (as they do for some companies in the last month of a quarter) receivables will be highest at the end of the quarter compared to the two earlier months in the quarter. DSO will normally be highest in the last month of the quarter compared to the two earlier month-ends regardless of what a credit manager does. Credit managers can, conversely, receive undue praise when sales are falling in a quarter.

While several methods are employed to offset the impact of fluctuating sales involving averaging sales and receivables, collection percentage is still my choice as I can explain changes easily to management. I still encourage the newcomer to explore the excellent discussions of DSO, including best possible and average cost of delinquency, available from the Credit Research Foundation, which is part of the National Association of Credit Management. These discussions include comparisons of credit performance done on a national or industry basis using various DSO formulas.

Another measure is *aging percentages*. Several aging categories are established, usually in 30-day increments. The most popular are current (0-30 days old), past due 1-30 days, past due 31-60 days, past due 61-90 days and over 90 days past due. The total for each category is computed as a percentage of the total receivables outstanding. Obviously, in a large sales month, the amount current will be a larger percentage of total receivables thus distorting the report. Over a period of time, at least six months, comparing the aging percentages in each aging category can prove to be worthwhile.

Bad debt write-offs as a percentage of sales is another numerical measure. The calculation is simple enough but it is difficult to find a company that is consistent with the timing of writing off an account.

In short, the numerical measures do provide a sense of what is going on, but they can't give us the full story of how a credit manager is doing. Donald Miller, former credit manager of Crown Zellerbach made perhaps the greatest advance in this area in his book, *Improving Credit Practice* (now out-of-print, unfortunately).

Mr. Miller said you had to look at:

1. The quality of information in the credit files of marginal accounts. How current is this information?
2. How promptly past-due accounts are followed-up determined by reviewing collection files.
3. Number and type of accounts restricted to cash terms.
4. A comparison of department expenses to budget. Where was the money spent?
5. Upgrading and training of the credit manager and his people.

While Mr. Miller's criteria for performance are more subjective, I think they are more valid than pure numbers. Numbers convey a sense of concreteness which simply isn't always present in credit work. Like the salesman, the credit manager works at developing customers, usually those who are unable or unwilling to pay promptly. His job is to help the sales department develop a strong base of good paying accounts. He does this by acquiring adequate information, cultivating friendships, taking calculated and prudent risks and conducting himself professionally at all times.

Here are the characteristics of four types of credit departments that you may find useful for evaluation purposes:

1. *Quasi.* Characterized by lack of a full-time credit manager, the quasi credit department reacts to situations as they become problems. This department is often buried deep within the accounting department and a junior accountant is given the part-time responsibility of telephoning past-due accounts. There is no credit approval process. That responsibility has been given to the sales department. Collection follow-up is sporadic. An aging of accounts receivable is usually done.

2. *Embryo.* This department is fortunate to have a full-time credit manager, although the person filling the position may not have been adequately trained. Collection work is the primary function of this department and it is done rather well. Credit approvals are done by the sales department although the credit manager may order reports from credit agencies to assist them.

3. *Mature.* A full-time qualified and trained credit manager heads this department. A credit approval system is in place: credit checks are performed before customer credit is accepted. Collection work is professional, systematic and effective. Disputes and complaints received from customers are promptly routed and followed-up until resolved. The credit manager prepares a monthly report for management which analyzes receivable investment and trends in the company and industry. The credit manager has established a good rapport with sales and financial management.

4. *Contributing.* This credit department effectively contributes to the progress of the company. Fully 80% of the credit manager's time is spent helping to select

new customers, cultivating friendships with the key personnel of the largest customers and training subordinates. The routine activities of credit approval and collection are handled by well-trained and competent assistants. The sales department considers their credit department an extension of their own, a function that helps them make credit sales that would not otherwise be prudently possible. The general manager is kept informed of problem situations on an exception basis.

This system of classification, if nothing else, may give credit managers some targets to shoot at.

Our final summary must necessarily get into some philosophy about the job of a credit manager. A company accepts the credit of customers in order to sell them. This job of selecting customers is an important one, for it costs a company a significant out-of-pocket amount to obtain a new account. If payments of new customers cannot be predicted, the company cannot predict how much profit it will make in sales (for accepting slow payment is really an involuntary price reduction), nor can it predict its own cash flow which it needs to remain solvent.

Any company must have in its customer base some marginal customers — customers who do not have the ability to pay within terms. The credit manager's job is to either convince these customers to pay promptly or obtain security to offset the risk of financial loss.

The credit manager is a manager of the cash flow of the company and is therefore concerned about how easy his company makes it for customers to pay. He pays particular attention to terms and conditions of sale, quotation forms, invoice documentation, cash gathering facilities such as lockboxes, collection follow-up programs and handling of complaints and disputes.

Above all, he must be a teacher and a leader. It's his job to motivate co-workers, customers and his people to adopt goals, strategies and techniques designed to raise sales volume toward its theoretical maximum within a predetermined bad debt write-off level and maximize cash inflows.

The job is dynamic and requires constant learning and training. Customers change their sources of supply as their needs change. Companies that do not sense and respond to these changing needs will soon find themselves out of business. Credit managers are no different.

On Becoming A Good Credit Manager

79

Many people have asked me what it takes to become a good credit manager. This is an extremely difficult question to answer, for credit managers, like most people, come in many shapes, sizes, with varying styles and different ways of approaching their job.

However, I believe I have discovered some common traits that run through successful credit managers.

- They approach their job with a positive attitude. They are convinced personally that what they do is important and they take their job very seriously. Given enough time, resources and management support, they feel there is no job they can't do and they enthusiastically sell the value of their job and responsibilities.
- They have taken the time to gain the technical knowledge they need to do their job in a professional way. Through courses in college, home study through the National Institute of Credit, Dun and Bradstreet, or seminars conducted by individuals and colleges, they attempt to learn the basics of credit management and strive to acquire knowledge in law, marketing, accounting, human resource management and basic management.
- They are creative and look for problems to solve in a new and perhaps more effective way. Through frequent interchange at group meetings conducted by their local affiliate of the National Association of Credit Management, they question other credit managers about

problems they have solved or have been unable to solve. When they are with their customers and sales people, they question the products, marketing strategy, image and strategies of their company in an attempt to solve problems and do things better.

- They are action-oriented. They get things done. Most make list after list, set priorities and then get about the job of achieving these goals. They reward themselves on their successes, admit their failures, pick themselves up and go again. Their energy seems unlimited.
- They train their people constantly. They know the knowledge they have is due in large measure to someone having taken the time to teach them and they in turn take the time from their busy day to help their people do a better job.
- Finally, they have humility. The job of credit management is so dynamic, so complex that they can never sit back and feel they have it made. Not only have computers revolutionized this profession, but changing attitudes of people and the increasing tempo of the 1980's have made the credit manager of today very different from his predecessor.

Credit managers are not really that different from other company managers. Each manager has his technical specialty and his special way of doing things, but the proven principles of management are fairly universal.

Good managers question why things are done, so a better way can be found. Good managers question themselves as to why they do what they do and whether what they do makes a significant contribution to their company. Good managers give their people the credit they deserve and attempt to place them in situations where they can be successful. Above all, good managers do the important things that management wants them to do and seek to learn constantly so they can do more.

You have taken a big step in your career by reading this book. Hopefully, the ideas presented will stimulate your thinking about what you do and why you do it. Not all these ideas will work for you. But if you gained one new idea and applied it to your work at your company, your effort will have been worth it.

As a reward for that effort, I will give you one more idea that has helped me. I have looked for a long time to summarize credit interchange data such as that presented in NACM reports into a shorthand code. This is the code I have developed which consists of three symbols:

First Position: Number of Suppliers Reporting

A — Over Ten
B — 6 to 10
C — 1 to 5
F — None

Second Position: Average High Credit Reported.

A — Over $100,000
B — $50,000 to $99,000
C — $10,000 to $49,000
D — $1,000 to $9,000
E — Under $1,000
F — None
Z — Cash Only

Third Position: General Manner of Payment

1 — Prompt within terms
2 — Slow not more than 1-30 days
3 — Slow 31-60 days
4 — Slow 61-90 days
5 — Slow over 90 days
8 — No payment trend determined
9 — Placed with attorney or agency

Using this shorthand code, you can tell quickly the results of payment experience. For example, an AB4 tells me over 10 suppliers report average high credit in excess of $50,000 each and the customer pays slow 61-90 days to most of them. You can insert this code into your electronic credit file discussed on page 69. You thus have a summary of the contents of the report without having to review the full report.

This system has worked well for me for over ten years. It seems to work with any credit interchange report. Try it! You may like it. The best of luck to you with your career in credit management.

Important Terms for Credit Managers

Credit management has its own terminology. Be certain you are familiar with the terms below. They are listed alphabetically and include the numbers of the chapters in which they are discussed.

Final Test

You may wish to test yourself to see how much you learned. This test is similar to the CRMA Certified Credit Representative Written Examination.

1. Define credit in as simple terms as possible. Structure your definition so that you place a burden on your customer, enabling you to deal more effectively with him.

2. Name three primary goals of a credit manager.

   a.

   b.

   c.

3. A well-designed credit application can be a most useful tool in collections. Discuss.

4. In choosing an information source, a credit manager considers three criteria. List each and discuss.

   a.

   b.

   c.

5. Identify the 5 C's of credit. Define each and then tell the purpose of using this acronym.

   a.

   b.

   c.

   d.

   e.

6. What is one of the most important pieces of information a credit manager can obtain about a prospective customer? How can it be confirmed as being correct. (Hint: In a retail credit scoring system based upon 100 points, this information can often count 50 points.)

7. Discuss the purpose of risk categories. How can this classification make management of a receivable portfolio more effective? Should more than five risk categories be used? Name and define the five used by the author.

8. Define a marginal account. We discussed use of the National Safety Council's Defensive Driving Formula as a method of approaching these accounts. Summarize the method.

9. Discuss the use of a personal guarantee to reduce risk from loss. To be most effective, what steps should a credit manager go through to use this device.

10. Tell how a stand-by letter of credit works. Why is the stand-by letter of credit useful to a company just starting in business?

11. In discussing credit information with other credit managers, the discussion should be limited to certain facts. What are they?

12. Does a credit manager prefer to set up an account in the name of an individual or a corporation? Discuss the different legal responsibilities of these forms of business organization.

13. What important information can a salesman provide a credit manager about a new account?

14. Many banks require an original signature on a written inquiry from a credit manager. Why?

15. Why does the author stress the importance of having a form documenting the credit approval signed by the credit manager?

16. How does a credit manager determine that a credit limit is large enough to satisfy the customer's purchase requirements?

17. What is the primary purpose of an invoice? Why should a credit manager become involved in its design?

18. Discuss the value in using a lockbox.

19. When reading an invoice, the customer will first focus his eyes on what part of the document? Identify this area and describe how the customer's eyes should travel down through the invoice, listing at least seven key pieces of information the customer should obtain.

20. If your management objected to changing the format of the invoice your company was presently using, what arguments would you give to attempt to sell your changes?

21. A standard collection process goes through five stages. Name each and describe how the attitude of the collector toward the customer changes dramatically between stage three and four.

22. The collector's objective in a collection call is to obtain a commitment from the customer, a commitment which includes three elements. What are they?

23. When should a collector refer handling to a third party?

24. Describe the differences in approach between collecting from an A or B credit risk than a D or E credit risk.

25. When a collector runs into a customer dispute, what are his three responsibilities?

26. Sales departments are often reluctant to issue credit memos. Describe the accounting entry that reflects the impact of a credit memo.

27. Describe the value of having an Exception Receivable Report which documents the customer's complaint.

28. Give the entries (debit and credit) that reflect the following transactions.

    a. A sale is made to a customer on net 30 day terms.

    b. A payment of $100 is received from a customer on his account.

    c. A cash sale of $400 is made.

    d. An account of $900 is written off as a bad debt.

    e. A credit memo of $120 is issued to a customer's account.

29. Assets are normally listed on the left-hand side of a balance sheet in order of ________. List the six most common asset accounts in the order in which they are listed.

30. Why does a balance sheet balance?

31. Define working capital. What does this tell you?

32. Tell how each of the following ratios are computed and what they can tell a credit manager about a customer's ability to pay within terms.

    a. Liquid Ratio

    b. Current Ratio

    c. Receivable Turn

    d. Inventory Turn

    e. Payable Turn

    f. Debt to Equity

33. Are audited financial statements the only valid presentation of financial data?

34. What item appears on both the balance sheet and profit loss statement?

35. Show how the cost of goods sold is calculated.

36. Why is a fiscal year-end statement more valuable than an interim statement?

37. Computers can reduce daily routine tasks credit managers perform. Give some examples.

38. The author mentioned that credit managers work in a symbol factory. Give some examples of coding schemes that simplify the credit manager's work.

39. Show how the following numerical measures of credit performance are calculated.

    a. Days Sales Outstanding

    b. Aging Percentages

    c. Collection Percentage

40. Which of the measures in question 39 appears to be the most useful? Why?

41. Discuss the particular benefits a credit manager can obtain from each of the following credit reports.

    a. Credit Interchange reports of affiliated associations of the National Association of Credit Management

    b. NACM Business Credit Reports

    c. Dun and Bradstreet Reports

42. Some companies involve their credit manager in the budgeting process especially in the preparation of the sales forecast. Describe.

43. How does one obtain the title credit manager?

44. Should a credit manager report to a controller? A sales manager? A treasurer? The company president? Discuss briefly.

45. Should business credit be subject to the same laws as consumer credit? Why or why not?

46. Why shouldn't responsible credit managers compile "black lists" of customers who don't pay, and distribute the lists to their friends?

47. Should every company support having a "contributing credit department"?

48. Why should a credit manager become involved in anything but collections? Isn't this what he gets paid for?

49. What factors should be considered by a credit manager in concurring with his company's decision to give special payment terms to a customer?

50. If you were credit manager of a credit department which included a senior credit analyst, credit clerk and department secretary, what types of training would you consider for each?